I0411958

Our Nation in Decline

Tom Hopper

ACKNOWLEDGEMENT

To my wonderful teacher wife Marilyn

TABLE OF CONTENTS
Our Nation in Decline

CHAPTER 1

Democracy in Jeopardy

Our Nation is in decline. Democracy is failing and the Democratic Republic of the United States of America is in jeopardy.

As citizens we have only ourselves to blame. We foolishly assumed that removing the yolk of autocracy would guarantee freedom. We did not realize that freedom requires even greater personal commitment to the nation. We did not participate in building the great nation we have. We ignored the concerns of the founders. Our malaise is responsible for the national decline.

Mr. Washington, we are humiliated that the nation you and your brave followers fought and died for did not live up to the greatness you exemplified.

Mr. Adams, we foolishly ignored your concern with the rise of political parties.

Mr. Jefferson, we are chastened that we did not listen to your concerns on the dangers of banking.

Mr. Franklin, your concern with whether we could keep the Republic was prophetic.

To all of the founders I hope we can save it.

Chapter 2

'the seeds of death are planted with birth'

The chapter title is intended to shock the reader. An old homily it was the somber expression of a former Information Technology colleague after evaluating a failing system.

The US Constitution was the birth of The United States of America. In a world of nations ruled primarily by monarchs the prophetic vision of a Democratic Republic governed by and for the people was a revolutionary governmental concept.

Were 'the seeds of death' planted in the Constitution?

When the founders gathered to create a new nation their primary objective was avoidance of a monarchy. They had just been freed from under the English yoke. Their major concerns were two major flaws of English law namely 'patronage' and 'inheritance' under which the colonies functioned prior to the creation of the new nation.

Patronage is a double-edged sword. As a true benefactor it has produced the world's great music and breakthroughs in science and technology. Patronage however becomes corruption when done with the expectation of payback. Despite the vehement concern of John Adam patronage was not addressed and the 'seeds of death' were planted. A 'spoils' disorder was the result. In the nations new institutional government positions were given to party associates dependent on their payback. The 'spoils' disorder was finally addressed and the Civil Service Act limited patronage at the lower levels of government.

The 'seeds' were not completely eliminated however and patronage is still the dominant force at the upper levels of government. My medical doctor a native of India expressed it; 'in India we have corruption and bribery, in the United States we have politics and campaign spending'.

Another concern with English law was inheritance. While the king's son inherited the throne, his gardener's son also inherited his position on the death of the father. Inheritance was the fundamental basis for leadership across the nation. Inheritance was a constraint on both citizens and the nation and the founders recognized this societal weakness.

The concern with inheritance was addressed and selection of leadership for the new nation was determined to be by the people. To provide leadership an electoral process was instituted. At that time eligible voters were white male citizens who owned twenty acres of land. The electoral process unfortunately has a mathematical flaw which allowed non-citizens to dominate elections as eligibility increased and campaign spending limits were raised. Most states consistently vote along party lines (the Red/Blue Syndrome) and the results can be predicted with high reliability. There are a few states that are not consistent and are defined euphemistically as 'swing' states. These states determine the winner of the national election. By pouring billions of campaign dollars into the swing states special interests can 'buy' the election for their party. This deviation was confirmed as an institutional flaw in 1960 when a wealthy citizen poured millions of dollars into his son's campaign. The mathematical flaw in the electoral process has become an institutional 'seed' failure. The swing state aberration effectively disenfranchises eighty five to ninety percent of the nation's citizens in selecting a chief executive.

A dominant failure of the electoral process is leadership selection. Selection of the chief executive has become a Hollywood style popularity contest whereby political parties pick candidates based on their chance of winning rather than their ability to manage the nation. Political parties then spend or (waste) billions of citizens dollars in the 'swing states' to elect their designate. The winning party then dominates the chief executive until the next election. This vacuous process has been an abysmal failure in providing competent chief executives for over two hundred years.

Another and probably more significant failure of the electoral process has allowed a tawdry political practice to embed itself in government. Completely embedded in government today, the patronage based political community controls the nation. Every national decision is first evaluated on its political impact; the welfare of the nation is secondary. Citizen voices have been stilled.

Patronage is the 'seeds' root factor of the nation's decline. The decline will continue until enlightened citizens accept that survival of the Democratic Republic is dependent on containment of this festering malady.

CHAPTER 3

The Institutional Government

An additional measure to address avoidance of a monarchy was creation of a 'balance of power' within the new government. A decision was made for an institutional structure in which a board of directors representing the people would provide primary governmental leadership. They were to define the procedures within which the nation would function and provide the necessary funding. A chief executive would manage day-to-day operations under the procedures and funding established by the board of directors. A mechanism was provided for a once a year 'State of the Union' feedback to the board of directors to identify executive concerns and request changes. A judiciary function was established to enforce the procedures established by the board of directors. That structural organizational concept was well ahead of its time and has been proven thousands of times in successful institutions from government to commerce.

Once a structural foundation for a new venture has been established the success whether government or commercial is dependent on leadership and the rules under which the organization will function. In commerce if either the rules or leadership is inadequate the venture fails and disappears. In Governments if the venture fails under any circumstance a new governmental system is adopted.

For the new nation the board of directors (Congress) was given primary constitutional responsibility to write the institutional rules (laws) upon which the nation would function. The fatal flaw was allowing Congress unrestricted authority to write their internal procedures as well as the rules (laws) to manage the nation. The patronage 'seed' ignored in the Constitution was actuated and the rules created were oriented more for congressional self-preservation than the good of the nation. Circumventing term limits a bumbling self-perpetuating Congressional hierarchy created a rambling and inadequate quagmire of rules (laws) to manage the nation.

The most significant failure in writing the rules (laws) for the new nation was the lack of precise definition of branch responsibilities and limits thereto. This failure created an institutional vacuum and the Chief Executive challenged Congress's constitutionally assigned Primary Governmental Role. The 'balance of power' so concerning to the founders was violated. The resultant power struggle between the legislative and the executive branches has been in existence since inception.

The nation has survived because the basic institutional structure was firm enough to avoid a complete split and there was enough dedicated leadership to allow the government to 'muddle through'. Today the tawdry political process now embedded in government has created such a vicious power struggle that cooperation between the branches has virtually ceased and the nations decline is accelerating.

Assuming adequate rules (Laws) have been developed the success of a venture is also dependent on leadership. In the commercial world leadership is developed through native ability, training and experience. The most capable leaders will rise to the top in their given field. In government leadership selection is based on the candidate's political commitment. The patronage 'seeds' are again actuated and inadequate leaders are assigned based on political payback. Mr. Adam's warning, that political parties were to be dreaded as the greatest evil under the Constitution, was fulfilled. For over two hundred years leadership candidates provided by the political process have been appalling.

Within the institutional government the embedded political parties have become more and more divisive. I'm sure the reader will agree that the ideology between the parties is not that far apart. The unconscionable tactics used by both parties to obtain power is a disgrace to the dedicated citizens of this great nation. Their despicable actions now threaten the very existence of the Democratic Republic.

Patronage based leadership is an abysmal failure in all branches. The result is an institutional government in stagnation. The 'seeds of death' danger to the nation has become undeniable.

CHAPTER 4

State-of-the-State

The 'seed' flaws have allowed the creation of an inadequate institutional government which has for over two centuries 'muddled through'. That 'muddling' has today reached epic proportions and if corrections are not made the current precipitous decline may well be the precursor to absolute failure.

Patronage as the root cause of governmental failure has never been addressed. The flaws have been there from inception but there have always been political procrastinators to provide a 'legal patch' such as the Civil Service Act. These politically oriented patches have allowed the nation to survive while the inexorable decline continues. For over two hundred years our nation has functioned under a constantly increasing quagmire of laws that has met every crisis with inadequate short-term solutions.

A political process prophetically forecasted by Adams as the greatest threat to the nation captured governmental power by convincing apathetic citizens that the Electoral Process is the epitome of democracy in action. The pageant theme was American exceptionalism, and the four-year Hollywood type extravaganza was the gambit that allowed the political process to gain control of the institutional government and ultimately the nation.

What was and should be a governmental model for all nations has become an electoral charade creating havoc on its citizens. A politically controlled government that should manage the nation quietly and professionally keeps citizens in a constant state of fear. Citizens are bombarded twenty-four hours a day with aggravated concerns such as the potential failure of Social Security to mask governmental failure.

The result is a government of shallow officials whose objectives are primarily self-preservation. This not a personal attack. There are good people in government who cannot function within a failing patronage based system. Those who are capable and committed throw up their hands and leave. The residue is the standing government. For readers who perceive that evaluation as radical or extreme I ask them to name five people in the federal government for whom they have complete confidence.

My long held view on this subject was confirmed in recent comments in a review of the Affordable Care Act. The architect identified Americans as stupid. His comments for which he later apologized reflect governmental perspective of mass citizen stupidity. I have long been concerned with citizen malaise but violently reject any connotation of citizens as stupid. My evaluation of citizens' perception of government is over-confidence. Confidence in government is a loyal attribute that was gained over centuries of trust. My concern is that trust was violated some time ago.

Over-confidence is dangerous. The comment on stupidity is a warning of the vacuity of a chaotic government grabbing at straws to perpetuate its existence. The 2000 page Affordable Care Act was an amateurish attempt to resolve a real problem but is unfortunately just another addition to the quagmire of laws perpetrated on the Democratic Republic for over two hundred years.

To emphasize the fragility of the current institutional government I have purposely avoided the obvious signs of decline such as the national debt and immigration. Exclusive of my evaluation of the electoral charade the nation is unquestionably in decline. The middle class has been virtually destroyed. Two jobs are required for the average family to exist while the quagmire of laws creates a privileged upper class. These are tentative problems brought about by an institutional government totally inadequate to manage this great nation.

Citizens I believe are beginning to recognize the decline whether or not they accept my appraisal of the electoral charade. Media poles consistently identify citizens concern with the national direction. The great American spirit is turning to dejection. Faith in government is lost.

This is a concise but precise definition of the State-of-the-State. The national decline will continue until citizens recognize the 'seeds-of-death' patronage malady and take corrective action to establish a capable institutional government.

CHAPTER 5

Restoring the Dream

Can democracy be saved? Has national decline reached the point of no return? Can the Democratic Republic be restored?

Restoring the Democratic Republic is not only possible but doable. The institutional government is structurally sound. The flaws have been identified and can be fixed. As a WWII combat veteran I was involved in the greatest national effort in the history of the world. The nation rose to a level of which even those involved could not believe. While there has been decline since that time our nation is still the most dynamic in the world with excellent technical resources. We still have the greatest power and wealth in the world. We have resilient citizens who will support restoration once they fully understand the need. The nation still has the necessary resources to 'muddle through' for a few decades while restoration is being done.

The caveat however is the will of the people. Citizen malaise, the focus of this book, must be overcome. Governmental attitude on citizen stupidity should not be taken lightly.

Restoring the dream will require a major national effort (project). The legal quagmire must be cleansed. Every institutional procedure must be analyzed for legitimacy and relationship to associated laws. Every institutional function must be reviewed for its relevance and operational effectiveness. Necessary organizational changes must be defined. Critical within this step is precise definition of institutional branch responsibilities.

Restoration will require a major national effort. To be successful the project must be outside of political domination or influence. Allowing the current political community to manage the project would be as an old homily says 'letting the fox loose in the henhouse'.

The project costs will be billions of dollars and must be funded and strongly supported by Congress as the primary government force. A board of directors should be selected from the most qualified citizens in the nation to audit and oversee the project.

There will be an ongoing conflict in establishing priorities and a dynamic project leader must have unrestricted authority. I suggest young readers review the career of Admiral Rickover whose dynamic leadership led the nation's development in nuclear submarines. A person of that stature will be required to lead the project. It will be the toughest job in the world within this century.

CHAPTER 6

Critique

So what have we learned? We have a structurally sound government in spite of a tentative balance of power. We have a failing institutional government because of inadequate laws and leadership. The institutional government has been embedded with a tawdry political process which effectively dominates the nation.

What was and should be a great nation is a disgrace to the dedicated citizens who have provided unequivocal national support through depressions and wars. I can't stop thinking of my buddies in European graves who died to perpetuate this electoral travesty.

As an avid follower of government and a retired pioneer in Computing and Information Technology I began the analysis of the nation's failure after the 2008 meltdown. The material presented in this book is based on the analysis for my two prior books on Fixing Government. USGOV.FIX was published in 2010 and updated in 2012 in anticipation of the national election. USGOV.REBUILD was published in 2013 with recommended fixes for both the institutional government and the economy.

The precipitous decline of the nation in the last six years has challenged me to continue my effort. The remainder of this book will be overviews of the factors leading to the decline. The overviews will be provided in a broad conversational perspective hopefully as a basis for a national dialogue. There will also be some suggested fixes from my prior books for discussion.

For those who feel that the 'seeds of death' portrayal is a little extreme my analysis confirms that Shock Therapy is required. This critique identifies a patronage based institutional government incapable of managing our great nation. The average citizen does not realize the fragility of the institutional government. The 2008 meltdown was a devastating warning. Citizens can continue the malaise and face the potential failure of their Democratic Republic or take corrective actions.

A national dialogue is critical.

Chapter 7

Patronage

Where do we grab this elephantine socio/economic enigma that has been the boon and bust for communities since civilization began?

Patronage is giving which is one of civilization's most valued phenomena. Giving is sharing which binds families and communities together. Common sharing is the prerequisite for a communal union, the basic elements for a nation's creation.

Why is patronage such a concern? The answer is the expectation when giving is done. True patronage is giving without expectation of payback. Giving with an expectation of payback whether implicit or explicit is the hidden menace. Implicit expectation implies a hoped-for but not unequivocal payback. Explicit patronage requires a specific payback.

The deleterious aspect of patronage is the transparent implicit or explicit agreement within which there is no audit trail. There is no contractual documentation and the acts are committed behind closed doors. The result for politics and ultimately for government is a hidden network of good-old-boys/girls who become the power brokers working outside the documented rules. This patronage based wheeling and dealing reaches into the depths of law making. There is no way of knowing the depth of these undocumented deals in our government but if the current stagnation is any measure it must be substantial.

Congressional failure to address patronage was one of the most lethal factors in the 'seeds' of the decline. I submit however that patronage can be contained and present the following example to support that position.

The Democratic Republic has a huge underground economy. Estimates approach two trillion dollars a year. If that economy were brought above-board our national funding problems would be solved. I studied this issue and provided a solution in my prior book USGOV.REBUILD. In any event this huge underground economy works quite well for its players. It operates within an implicit audit trail, and its financial base is suitcases of one hundred bills. It is a patronage-based system within which members function within well understood but undocumented procedures.

Deviations are limited and violators are dealt sternly within the system.

Patronage is a fascinating subject for discussion. The theory behind the entire spectrum and its implication to government and the possibility of a working socio/economic is in order. All governments except possibly the theocracies are subject to the same malady.

Can our failing patronage based Democratic Republic reach maturity? There is no guarantee of survival.

CHAPTER 8

Representation

Above all else the key element for restoration of the Democratic Republic is the return of citizen representation.

Obscured by centuries of political miasma our Democratic Republic is an institutional democracy within which all citizens are meant to participate equally either directly or through elected representatives. Citizens are the foundation of the republic and they (and only they) should determine the rules under which they will be governed.

Representation in the early years of the nation was characterized by significant citizen involvement through town meetings. With the increase in wealth and power citizen malaise developed allowing political parties through the electoral process to control elections. The political community then embedded itself in the institutional government, and today it completely rules the nation.

Citizen representation has been usurped by special interests. Those who follow government and the political process will immediately think of two brothers who own and manage a huge industrial empire. Actually they are only the tip of the iceberg. There are several hundred special interest groups. It would require an additional book to identify the various entities involved and their platforms.

In direct violation of democratic principles special interests now have greater representation than citizens. They control the political community that dominates government. That untenable position is supported by a recent Supreme Court ruling on campaign spending. Attempts by Congress to restore the people to primary representation was defeated, another devastating example of patronage's domination over the institutional government.

Citizens' only representation is through national elections, and the 'swing state' phenomenon disenfranchises about 85% to 90% of the population. The only direct representation citizens have at this time is election of their district's candidate to the House of Representatives. The House, which should be the dominant voice in representing the people, is a congressional stepchild with little clout. House elections are absurd formalities wherein the same members are elected every two years. With no term limits, they blindly follow their political leaders and continue until eligible for pensions.

The Senate, which is completely dominated by the political process, has virtually all law making power. Representation has been effectively lost through citizen malaise.

Citizens have virtually no say in how their government works. Democracy and a Democratic Republic can only be realized with complete and absolute citizen representation.

It can 'never' be achieved without it.

CHAPTER 9

The Electoral Process

The Electoral process is a major institutional cause of the nation's decline. The background was provided in Chapter 2.

The state based (red and blue) 'swing state' process has been a long-term controversy. By pumping billions of campaign dollars into a few 'swing' states the future of the nation is sold to the highest bidder. This was essentially proven in the 1960 election. As a student of government and a voter in that election I remember my shock when citizens did not realize the significance of that event. It was the undisputable manifestation of patronage's domination of the institutional government.

Those supporting the electoral process contend that a change would not have a significant impact on the election. Either by intent or ignorance that contention completely misses the point. The electoral process has virtually destroyed citizen selection of the nation's leadership.

Elections are the lifeblood of citizen participation and presidential elections are the focal point. The electoral process is citizens only means of representation and Congressional Districts are their only power source. To eliminate the swing state syndrome the recommendation in my second book was to elect the chief executive based on the number of Congressional Districts won. Using congressional districts as the electoral base would put local representatives who are now Congressional stepchildren at the forefront of government. District Representatives would become dynamic fighters for their executive choice and create greater voter involvement. Strengthening local involvement would bolster governmental structure and minimize political clout. Having to reach 435 districts rather than a few swing states would minimize political corruption.

A popular vote for the chief executive has been discussed but would be a tragedy. The tawdry political process would combat ethnic and other groups against each other and splinter what is left of the great American spirit.

Readers may have alternative recommendations but by whatever means necessary the red/blue 'swing state' cancer must be eliminated. The Electoral Process was and is the 'seed of death' for the Democratic Republic.

CHAPTER 10

The Quagmire of Laws

The 'quagmire of laws' is not just author-created jargon.

Laws are the lifeblood upon which both the moral and socio/economic elements of the nation function. The precision of its laws constitutes the quality of life factor for citizens. No one knows the degree of the quagmire within our nation but the current stagnation is an undeniable indicator of its depth.

Consider major institutional decisions such as regulating commerce with foreign nations. The decisions (or lack of) when industry was sending jobs overseas was unquestionably a major factor in the nations decline. Congress, which has the responsibility for regulating commerce, did nothing. Government stood idly by while massive wealth creating jobs were eliminated at home and sent to other nations. The incongruity of this specific default is the forfeiture of our nation's wealth provided the seed money for China's explosive growth who now challenge our nation as world leader.

This is only one example of the myriad of inadequate laws upon which the nation has functioned for over 200 years. Our laws both proactive and reactive are simply not adequate. Tackling the quagmire will be a major factor in restoration and will require the highest quality of the nation's Legal and Information Technology expertise.

The legal quagmire is real and is the fragmented base of the institutional government. Its danger to the nation cannot be over emphasized.

CHAPTER 11

Leadership

How do other nations select leadership? There are models of every type.

Switzerland has updated their Constitution (laws) for 600 years and have developed a mature democratic nation within several spoken languages. Norway, a democratic constitutional monarchy, is probably the best-managed nation in the world. China, which is theoretically a communist nation, is governed by an oligarchy. Most parliamentary nations are fighting stagnation. The Middle East theocracies continue centuries of turmoil. Japan is coming out of twenty years of stagnation but is already facing a recession. Russia is returning to an autocracy. Virtually every nation in the world is striving for a better government and leadership is the critical component.

How can our nation improve leadership? In commerce there is a migration path within which individuals can develop leadership skills and advance through levels of responsibility dependent on their abilities. The better performers will rise to the top. Within an electoral process that creates constant management reshuffling there is no logical migration path.

How can our nation attain a commercial level of leadership within an institution built on patronage? Containment of patronage is critical and should provide an answer. Within the new Information Technology profession there are all sorts of modeling and simulation tools that can be used.

Developing improved leadership is possible if the best minds in the nation are brought to bear and a committed national effort is made.

Chapter 12

The Judiciary

I am going to recapitulate my judiciary evaluation from my original book. I hope the reader will accept it in the spirit written.

There is a phenomenon in most professions whereby the developers create a unique language to insulate their particular methodology. I observed this as a pioneer in the computer field. As the world's second oldest profession, the legal community is a glaring example; citizens are dependent on whereas and wherefore in all matters of law.

The nation has been dominated from its inception by the legal community, with roughly 40% in the House and 60% in the more powerful Senate. The quagmire of laws is the result. The efficacy of the judiciary is directly dependent on the quality of the law making process. With precise laws adjudication can be quick and final. With poorly written laws adjudication can be time consuming and often fruitless. The obscure danger of poorly written laws is the highest court becomes the nation's default lawmaker.

I'm sure the legal quagmire costing by my rough estimate an average of five thousand dollars a year for each family is not purposely created or sustained. Less TV ads imploring citizens to sue for imaginary aches and pains would make me more comfortable. Tort reform, which should have been enacted decades ago, would increase my comfort level even more. A new law-making paradigm based on Boolean Logic (true or false) might even make me happy.

Recent decisions by the Supreme Court on campaign funding disenfranchising citizen representation should be a red flag as to the vacuity of the current judicial function.

Properly done restoration could elevate the judiciary to the honorable status given it in the Constitution.

CHAPTER 13

The Decline in Education

There is probably no greater failure in the national decline than in education. The United States became the wealthiest and most powerful nation in history with the best education system in the world. The founders realized that an educated population was necessary if the Democratic Republic was to become a reality. After the Constitutional Convention, John Adams went home and founded UMass. Jefferson went home and founded UV. Franklin went home and founded UPENN. One might wonder if Franklin's prophetic 'if you can keep it' remark on the Republic might have reflected his concern with education.

The educational system has either gotten lost or been the blind leader in the patronage/political disorder. Irrespective of the horror stories on primary and secondary test scores the most significant factor in my study was the degree of inadequacy as the level of education increased. Graduate levels have completely lost their educational perspective. Professionally mature disciplines should be taught within the rules of their functions. Putting together non-professional courses to attract or allow frivolous degrees is not education.

A glaring failure of educational inadequacy is to provide technical and advisory support to government. Government is the largest employer in the nation with unlimited opportunities. I was amazed to find roughly 1200 graduate level departments with degrees in Politics and Government. Placing the term Politics before Government as a course title is a disturbing indicator of educational mind-set. It is perhaps more significant as a substantiating indicator of the patronage malady which is destroying the nation.

With banking relatively unscathed from their 2008 dereliction the number of graduates moving to Wall Street to continue the frivolous financial practices leading to the meltdown is frightening. Banks are still the most powerful force in the nation with little government control. Another meltdown would almost surely cause national bankruptcy.

The educational process is a mirror image of the nation's decline and perhaps its precursor. Leading institutions have left education to establish their authoritative demeanor in all matters of human discipline.

One would wonder if the roughly trillion-dollar a year national investment in education is well spent. The restoration project will be an excellent sounding board for evaluation of the educational universe and their place in a true Democratic Republic.

CHAPTER 14

Banking

In the 1960's driving to visit my children in Connecticut I passed a striking new glass enclosed building. It was one of the New York City Banks. As an original computer geek my observation at that time was 'why are banks building huge centers when all the banking in the nation could be handled by one super computer'? The answer was provided forty years later when governmental oversight allowed the financial community to create banks to big to fail.

Money was established as a unit of measure for bartering. It was intended to represent the value of the unit being bartered. It eventually led to a unit of exchange for commerce. As commerce increased houses for handling money were established and borrowing was established as a mechanism to provide growth.

I am reminded of a resourceful monarch who called in the nation's coins and had them reminted with less silver to increase his wealth. That same objective has been met in our nation with a new minting method called printing presses. Due to lack of control by government and spurious political decisions, money that was intended to be supported by real value has been watered down. Money went from a unit of measure to a commodity and banks violated every principle of monetary discipline in its use. There had to be a meltdown and in 2008 the worst banking debacle in history nearly bankrupted the Democratic Republic. The nation's middle class was virtually destroyed. It was the most catastrophic financial disaster in the nation's history.

With the exception of senseless wars killing and maiming our children, it was the government's greatest citizen abuse in the nation's history.

The frightening aspect of the meltdown is that banks are still there and are posting huge profits while paying billions of dollars in titular fines for their 2008 transgressions. Patronage has allowed the perpetrators to go unpunished. The Dodd/Frank bill supposedly to strengthen control over banking is being recognized as the vacuous law it is. As of this date (12/14) there is an attempt in Congress to modify the law to allow banks more trading relief.

Is there is no limit to the audacity of patronage?

There is a fundamental requirement for any system and that is balance. Due to political takeover of government and the 2008 meltdown the middle class has been virtually destroyed and the nation's wealth has been consolidated within a small percentage of the population. This is an extremely dangerous condition. A solid middle class is a necessary socio/economic base for any nation. No nation has ever survived where power (money) has been consolidated by a privileged few. Unlimited campaign funding, now supported by the Supreme Court, is increasing that danger. Citizen representation almost completely lost today will disappear completely if it continues.

Money is supposedly the representation of the nation's wealth. The frivolous practices of the financial community and the irresponsibility of government in controlling the value of our currency have destroyed the confidence of its citizens. With some expertise in Information Technology, I can foresee the financial community as a national utility. Every banking function can be done with a sophisticated national computer based network. As a matter of fact all the nation's banks are already networked. Nationalization has been discussed in the past but avoided as a potential inhibition to the nation's free enterprise system. If the financial community does not stop their frivolous practices, nationalization may very well become a necessity.

If there were no other reason for governmental restoration the need to get our financial community under control would justify the effort. The nation has a fragile financial base. Bankruptcy is a constant danger and can only be guaranteed when an adequate institutional government is in place.

The 'seeds of death' danger for the Democratic Republic is most significant in the financial community and should be a major factor in restoration.

CHAPTER 15

Congress

The Constitutional role given Congress was to represent the people and translate their requirements into a working set of (laws) upon which the government could function. Giving them 'unlimited' primary government authority was the 'seeds of death' planted by the Constitution. I was particularly shocked by the magnitude of Congressional failure in that many of the founders were actively involved in government for the early years of the nation.

Why was the magnificent vision eviscerated? The answer is of course Congress.

With Constitutional carte blanche Congress violated every sense of responsibility to the new nation. By avoiding term limits Congress has grown into a ingrained cult of self-serving puppets whose primary objective is self- preservation. As the primary governmental force Congress is totally inadequate to manage the nation of today. A mature Democratic

Republic can never be attained if their abysmal performance is allowed to continue. Their role must be
reevaluated and redefined. I make no excuses for this
evaluation, citizen ratings of this pathetic branch of
government is testimony enough.

Critical for Congress is the organizational structure. To
have the primary government law-making body split
by political ideology challenges all reason or logic. It
virtually guarantees confrontation in an organization
whose single objective should be for the good of the
union. A logical organization would be by States and
Districts, which are the national base. A single speak-
er could be elected to manage law-making process
based on proven rules of order. Some ideological
concessions could be allowed through shared committee assignments.

Is a bicameral organization necessary? Are two bodies
a necessary requirement for law making? The Senate
is the power base for the nation and is completely
dominated by the political process. The House is a
congressional stepchild with no real clout. Their two-
year terms are absurd. Would not a single representa-
tive body with a super committee review prior to bills
moving to the chief executive be more effective?

Hard procedural time-based rules for handling new legislation devoid of ideological constraint should be implemented. For political leaders to be able to impede legislation in any way is a violation of democratic principles.

Congress is the major cause of the national decline. The electoral sideshow has perpetuated their existence. If the purpose was to create citizen malaise, it worked? With no term limits citizens return the same inadequate members every election. None of us are absolved from that responsibility for the national decline.

Restoration must reevaluate Congress and completely redefine their function. Further comments on that vacuous organization would be a waste of the reader's time.

CHAPTER 16

The Chief Executive

The executive role has been the key element in the development of the new nation. After Congress initial failure to carry out their constitutional governmental responsibility, the Chief Executive challenged primary power. The nation then developed around the ideology and the weakness or strength of the chief executive. A brief historical review is in order.

After the initial years a wrathful Andrew Jackson created a storm of controversy including shutting down the national bank. Muddlers were the norm until Lincoln freed a million slaves at the cost of six hundred thousand American lives. The result was one hundred years of humiliation for the former slaves and the creation of a racist society struggling with the aftermath that continues to this day. Muddlers continued until Theodore Roosevelt recognized the danger of a plutocracy and brought the industrial community under control. A major executive challenge was the great depression of the 1930's. Prior to that time social and economic functions were somewhat isolated. With the nation in turmoil the chief executive became more powerful and a new socio-economic paradigm was created. It was called the New Deal and was the formalization of social reforms.

In WWII the nation created great wealth and became the undisputed world power. Following the war living was easy and the nation entered a period of malaise. The ultimate caveat of patronage allowed a wealthy citizen to buy the presidency for his son. The political process provided a constant string of incompetent executives. The last fifty years of executive incompetence has resulted in useless and unnecessary wars killing and maiming our children, virtual elimination of the middle class, and crushing debt.

The final precipitous step in executive decline was in the new century. A pointless war possibly the most dangerous executive decision in history was initiated at massive costs and subsequent potential danger to the nation and the world. Executive dereliction is in no way negated by the fact that an incompetent Congress supported that travesty.

Recovery from the costs of war was exacerbated by a banking dereliction that nearly caused governmental bankruptcy and virtually destroyed the nation's middle class. Two centuries of the nation's institutional flaws were coalesced almost immediately into virtual governmental stagnation. Ideology was not a significant factor; both parties share in the blame.

The purpose of this evaluation is not to deride pathetic executive performance, rather to emphasize that all were/are the result of patronage and a tawdry political process.

Restoration will require a reevaluation of executive responsibility. The 'seeds' constitutional vacuum allowing the escalation of executive power was unquestionably a major factor in the nation's decline.

CHAPTER 17

The Election Syndrome

As a talking point for discussion I submit the following.

My definition of our government's institutional system is an electoral charade. A supposedly democratic nation is dominated by a pseudo-monarchical chief executive. The group that was given primary governmental authority has morphed into rambling incoherent assemblage using vague ideology to continue their existence. This pathetic excuse for an institutional government is perpetuated by self-made rules initiated 225 years ago and continued through political, legislative, and executive incompetence.

National elections are the input and major source of power for our institutional government. My analysis shows that what should be an orderly process has been turned into a carnival exercise controlled by the political process. Election scheduling established in the 18th century is today a disturbance to both government and the economy. Major decisions are delayed because of potential impact on the next election. These delaying disturbances have accelerated as the political establishment increased its domination of government and political concerns precede those of national governance.

There is a secondary disturbance caused by election scheduling. A major administration change in the first four-year presidential election can send the nation into a socio/economic tailspin. The second term presidential election while not as significant can still provide a substantial disturbance. Major changes in Congress can exacerbate the disturbances in either case.

These disturbances, along with previously defined concerns, could be rectified with improved scheduling and minor changes to the current institutional structure. To address these disturbances I am going to recapitulate the findings and recommended institutional fixes defined in my second book. These 'fixes' were based on the same analysis the reader has just gone through.

First is to change the Presidency to a single seven-year term. Divided terms add substantially to election disturbances. This was recommended in my 2010 book.

Next is to change the Presidential winner based on Congressional Districts vs the red/blue swing state syndrome. This was covered in both of my previous books.

Next was to limit campaign contributions to electors only. This was discussed in Chapter 9. Citizens are the democratic base for the nation. Unlimited campaign spending has exacerbated the electoral charade.

Next was to extend the term of House members to six years.

Next was to limit all Congressional members to two terms.

Next to have elections for both House and Senate every two years for one third of the members.

Last to prohibit retired members of Congress from becoming lobbyists.

These recommended changes with a restructuring of Congress by State and District would substantially minimize political clout and begin the containment of the patronage cancer.

I hope these discussion points will be helpful.

CHAPTER 18

Recapitulation

Is the old guy trying to scare citizens with his 'seeds-of-death' warnings?

I have purposely avoided the current signs of national decline to concentrate on the basic governmental flaws. Even with the decline following WWII we finished the last century the wealthiest nation in the world with low unemployment. The national debt was in a reasonable relationship to GDP and we had a solid middle class.

We entered the new century reasonably healthy and then saw the nation torn to shreds by the tawdry political process. The 'seeds of death' flaws, which were gradually destroying the nation, coalesced in two administrations into the greatest setback in history. The nation today is institutionally weaker than during the great depression, the low point in prior history. Ideology cannot be a factor. The tawdry political process and citizen malaise share the decline.

The nation can continue the electoral charade at its jeopardy. The current institutional government is totally inadequate to manage the nation. The portents for the 2016 election are continuation of the charade. If nothing is changed the nation faces at least six and probably ten years of continued institutional inadequacy.

What are the options? A restoration project if approved will require three to five years of analysis and five to ten years of implementation dependent on political and public support. There might be some short term restorative options if the institutional fixes identified in Chapter 17 could be implemented without endangering the final solution. The best hoped for turn-around of the pathetic government of today is probably the early 2030's.

That is, IF WE START TODAY.

Citizens can put their heads in the sand and hope that the nation can continue to function as is. My personal opinion, based on seventy five years of governmental observation and six years of analysis, is that another sixteen years as destructive as the last might make restoration a moot point. We could have passed the point of no return.

Don't say you weren't warned.